# Dive Theory for Your Sc Open Water Course

Prepare and spend more time diving and less in the classroom during your diving course for beginners of recreational diving

Marc Luxen

ISBN: 9781980960881

This is the theory that you need to know for your open water course. In the manual you will get during your open water course there are questions you need to answer. The knowledge you need to answer these questions is in this little book. It is presented in same order as the questions, in short paragraphs. This way, you can prepare at home and spend less time on theory during your holiday.

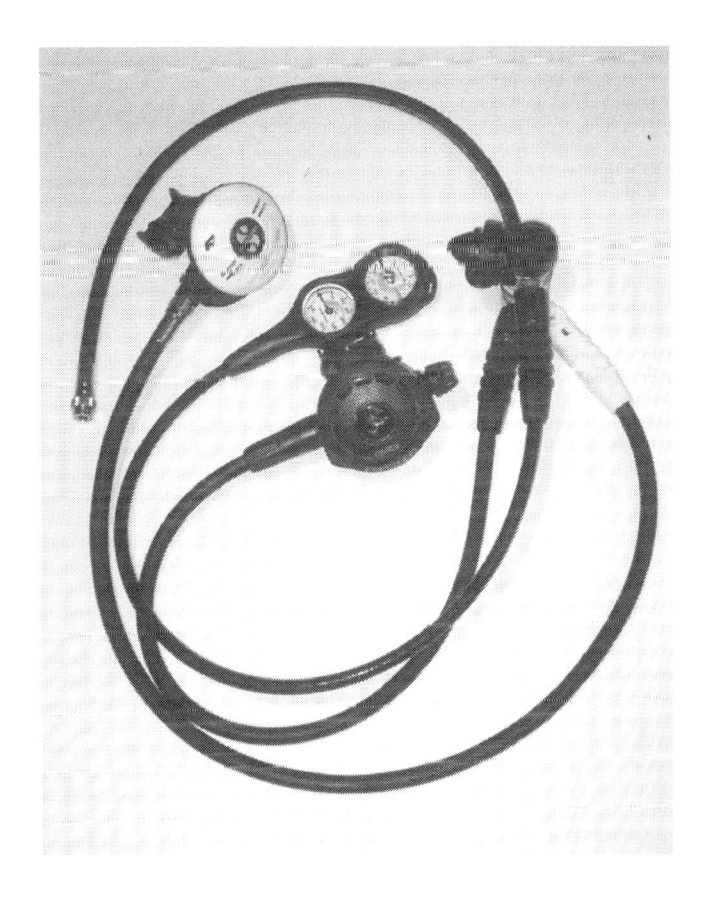

Let's first have a look at the equipment.

Regulator: The thing your breath from. The first stage you attach to your tank, the second stage you hold in your mouth.

BCD: Buoyancy Control Device, a vest that holds your tank and that you can inflate and deflate. Fins, Mask, Snorkel and Weight belt you know already

Water weighs much more than air. That is because water is much denser than air. When you go up or down ten meters on land, you do not notice anything. The pressure change is almost nothing. But when you go up or down ten meters in the water, the pressure becomes very different. When you are on the surface, the air that presses on you weighs 1 bar

|  | Seawater | | Freshwater | |
| --- | --- | --- | --- | --- |
|  | Gauge | Ambient / absolute | Gauge | Ambient / absolute |
|  | 0.0 BAR | 1.0 BAR | 0.0 BAR | 1.0 BAR |
| 5 m | 0.5 BAR | 1.5 BAR | 0.49 BAR | 1.49 BAR |
| 10 m | 1.0 BAR | 2.0 BAR | 0.97 BAR | 1.97 BAR |
| 15 m | 1.5 BAR | 2.5 BAR | 1.46 BAR | 2.46 BAR |
| 20 m | 2.0 BAR | 3.0 BAR | 1.94 BAR | 2.94 BAR |
| 25 m | 2.5 BAR | 3.5 BAR | 2.43 BAR | 3.43 BAR |

Sea water is much heavier: it weighs 1 bar per ten meter. So if you go down 10 meters, the pressure there is 1 bar from the air, and also 1 bar from the water. The pressure at 10 meters depth is thus 2 bar: 1 of the air plus 1 of the water. You can now determine the pressure at each depth: 1 bar for every ten meters of water, and then 1 bar extra of the air. In fresh water it is something else, but you do not have to work with it now.

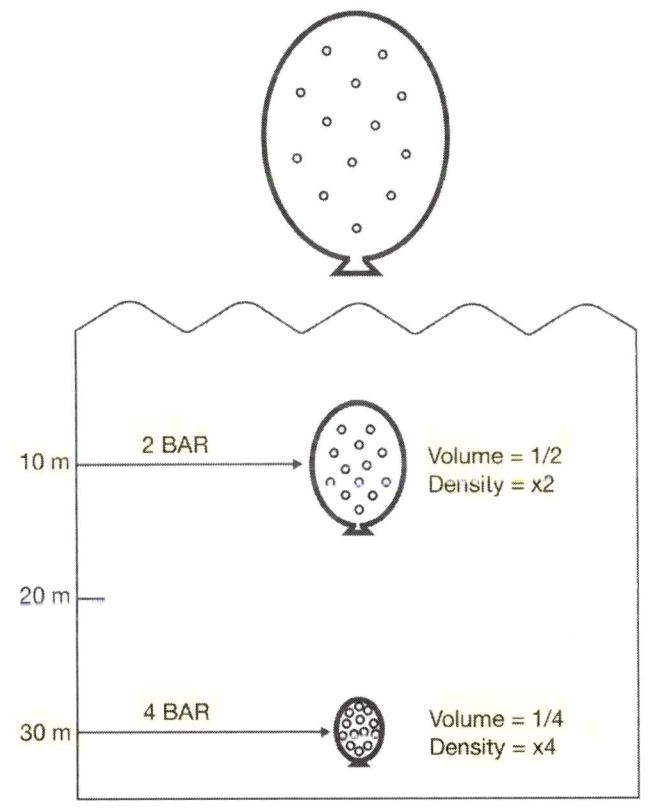

*Figure: A balloon at the surface, then at 10 m depth (2 BAR, Volume = 1/2, Density = x2), and at 30 m depth (4 BAR, Volume = 1/4, Density = x4).*

If you blow up a balloon before diving, and you take it down with you, it becomes smaller, because the water compresses the air in the balloon. How much smaller? That is fortunately easy. when the pressure is twice as large, the balloon becomes twice as small (1/2) And when the pressure is three times as large (at 20 meters), the balloon is three times smaller (1/3).

But of course there is still just as much air in the balloon, the air is only compressed by the water pressure. The density of the air in the balloon will therefore go up when you go down. How much denser is also easy: when the pressure is two bar (10 meters depth), then the balloon is twice as small as it was on the surface. The air therefore only has half the space, so the air in the balloon is twice as dense as on the surface. When the pressure becomes twice as large, the volume becomes twice as small and the density twice as large.

To prevent feeling pain in your ears when you go down, you need to add air. You have to equalise. You've probably done that in the mountains or on the plane. Some people swallow, and that's enough. Others wiggle with their jaw. But the most common way under water is to squeeze your nose, and then gently breathe out against your nose. You then squeeze some air into your ears and into your forehead cavities, you feel: pfffff. And of course you can also try all three methods at once.

What should you do if you are too late with equalising, or you do not succeed, and you feel pain in your ears? Whatever you do, do not try to blow harder and just continue. No, you have to sign to your buddy, go up a bit like a meter or so, and try equalising again. You do not have to go all the way back to the surface. Still doesn't work? Go up again a meter and try again. And when you succeed, you go down again.

When you go down on your first dive, you slowly go down, over the bottom or along a rope, so you can practice with equalising. You clear before you feel what, and at least every meter.

When you go up again, the pressure of the water becomes less and less. The air in your body escapes all by itself, you do not have to do anything. Sometimes however, people go diving when they have a cold. Going down has succeeded, but during the dive mucus was formed in your forehead cavities. The air in your body is then blocked, and cannot escape. The chance of this happening is greater if you have used anti-cold medicines. That is painful and can be dangerous at times. Do not dive if you have a cold, and certainly not with cold medication.

Now we are going to talk about the air in your lungs, and the most important rule when diving. Suppose we go down with an empty balloon, to ten meters. The pressure there is 2 bar. We blow that balloon up with our tank, completely full. Now we are going up. The pressure of the water is decreasing, and the balloon is getting bigger and bigger, until it explodes. Your lungs are two balloons that you fill up every time you breathe. What happens when you breathe, hold your breath, and then swim up? The air in your lungs continues to expand until something breaks. Fortunately it is very easy to avoid: NEVER HOLD YOUR BREATH! THIS IS THE MOST IMPORTANT RULE IN DIVING.

That is why your instructor asks you to blow bubbles when you do not have your regulator in your mouth! This way we can see that you do not hold your breath.

When you feel pain in your ears while you are going up, the solution is simple. You stop going up, you go down a bit and let the air slowly escape. That is one of the reasons why we always stop diving while your tank is still a quarter full. This way you have plenty of time to solve such problems.

You have seen that the pressure goes up when you go down. At 10 meters the pressure was 2 bar, so you breathe air with a pressure of two bar, twice as much as on the surface. You get twice as much air in your lungs, and your tank empties twice as fast as on the surface. At 20 meters it is even three times as fast.

If you exercise a lot under water, you may get out of breath. That is not good, because then you panic faster, and of course your air empties much faster. Just stop what you are doing, and start breathing slowly and deeply, until everything is back to normal. Then you can continue your dive.

Why does a steel ship float, and does a nail sink? This has to do with buoyancy. Whether you float or sink has to do with how much water you displace and how much you weigh yourself. When the water that you displace weighs more than you, you float. You have positive buoyancy. When the water you displace weighs less than you, you sink. You have negative buoyancy. And when the water you displace weighs the same as you weigh, then you hover: you do not sink and you do not float. You have neutral buoyancy. This is what you want when you are diving. You've probably seen pictures of people reading the newspaper in the Dead Sea, which is very salty. They float very easily. There is salt in salt water, so it weighs more than fresh water. The water you displace weighs more, and so you float easier in salt water than in fresh water.

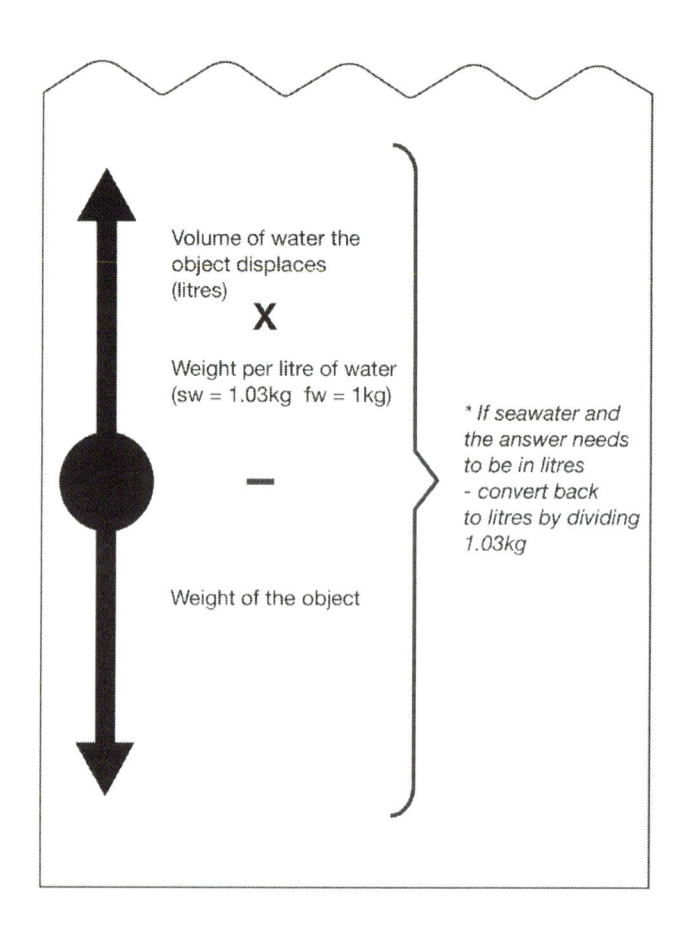

```
        Volume of water the
        object displaces
        (litres)
              X
        Weight per litre of water    * If seawater and
        (sw = 1.03kg  fw = 1kg)       the answer needs
                                      to be in litres
              −                       - convert back
                                      to litres by dividing
                                      1.03kg
        Weight of the object
```

You always dive with a buddy. This is mainly for safety, because you can always help each other and prevent mistakes. Of course it is also more practical and more fun.

If you are going to buy diving equipment, it is important that it is suitable for you personally and the dives you are going to make. In cold water you need a thick wetsuit for example. A second important consideration is that everything fits well. A third consideration is that it is also comfortable enough to wear an hour or more. Especially the latter can only be determined by you.

It is of course important to maintain your dive set properly. Your regulator is the most important part of your equipment. As soon as you notice that it is not breathing properly, you have to take it to a maintenance station.

There are two systems to screw your regulator onto your tank. The first is widely used in Europe and is the DIN system, where you can screw the regulator into the tank. In the rest of the world we use the International Connection System, a yoke system then with a clamp and a screw fits over the tank. Both systems are incompatible.

The most important skill in diving is controlling your buoyancy. You always want to have neutral buoyancy. As you go deeper, your suit is compressed, and your buoyancy gets more negative, when you go up, of course, the opposite happens. That is why you always adjust your buoyancy through your BCD when necessary.

**Refraction**

**Without refraction**

**With refraction**

Actual  Perceived

The path of light bends as it passes from the water to the air in your mask.

Mask lense

Because the path of light bends or 'refracts' objects appear approximately 33% and 25% closer in water than they do in air.

You've probably used a glass of water as a magnifying glass. When you are diving your mask works the same way. Things seem 33% larger under water, and therefore closer. You have to get used to it in the beginning. So: when you are back from diving on Koh Tao, do not lie about the size of the fish you have seen. They were smaller than you thought! Colours also disappear because the water absorbs them. At first red goes away, and then every colour of the rainbow in the same order, until only blue is left.

Water resists you when you try to move, much more than air. Swimming goes much slower than walking! You must therefore ensure that you are well-streamlined and do not move too fast. You will see that your dive instructor is hardly moving, you will occasionally see a fin go back and forth. You need to learn as soon as possible not to use your hands.

If you get cold under water, you cannot do much else than stop the dive, go up and find a warm spot. You do not want to go on shivering and teeth chattering: that is first and foremost very annoying and secondly you will panic much faster if something unexpected happens.

Because water has such high resistance, you can get tired quickly, especially when there is a lot of current. To avoid getting exhausted you have to know your own limits and always take it easy. And do not give in to the temptation to use your arms too! If you have not done all that and you have become very tired, then you do not have to go upstairs either. You may be able to hold onto a rock or sit on the bottom. Control your breathing, slowly and deeply, until you can continue. If you get very tired on the surface before or after your dive, you probably have not inflated your BCD. Do that right away and take it slowly.

During diving you always have one or more buddies with you. That is safer, and it is also easier and more fun, because you can help each other. It is always your own responsibility to stay with your buddy. But what do you do if you lose your buddy under water? The rule is: one minute search, and then go to the surface. If you were diving with more than 1 buddy, and there is 1 buddy lost, you stay with the other and you search together for 1 minute, and then you go to the surface.

Before you go scuba diving, speak to your buddy when you are halfway with your air, so that you can turn around and return to your starting point. But halfway through your air is not halfway through your tank, because you always want to get up with a quarter tank. You also have to calculate air for the ascent. Usually you estimate 20 bar for that. That means that 50 + 20 = 70 bar is needed at the end of the dive. So you have to deduct that from your full tank. You can use half of the rest to swim away, and half to come back. An example: you start with 200 bar. You need 50 bar reserve, and 20 to get up, so 70 in total. 200 bar minus 70 bar is 130 bar. That 130 bar you can divide over your dive, back and forth, so 130 divided by two, is 65 bar for the way, and 65 bar for the way back.

At the beginning and end of the dive you are on the surface. It is a good idea to ensure that you have always inflated your BCD, your mask on and your regulator in your mouth. Of course, the buddy system also still applies to the surface. So you are always prepared for high waves, or any unexpected situation.

You are about to start your dive. Of course you do not just go underwater right away, but you follow a five-step procedure, so that everything is checked. Use this mnemonic for this:

SORTED: Signal, Orientation, Regulator, Time, Equalize and Descend

This way you always do everything in the right order: 1) You signal to your buddy, 2) you see where you are and where you want to go, 3) you change your snorkel to your machine, 4) you check the time or your computer, you let your BCD trimmed (BCD) and 5) you start with equalising. And always in that order.

In water you cool down much faster than in air. The water in the tropics is around 28 degrees, but many people still wear a wetsuit. A wetsuit works by holding a layer of water between the suit and your skin to limit the flow. The air bubbles in the material itself of a wetsuit also provide additional insulation, but these bubbles are of course being compressed when you go down, and then your suit insulates a bit less. And this also means that your wetsuit gets less and less buoyancy as you go deeper. You need to adjust your buoyancy by putting small amounts of air in your BCD.

You can descend along a line, along the bottom, or in the water without reference point. It is better to use the coast or a line, because then you cannot become disoriented and dizzy, but it is not necessary.

Now let's talk about going up again at the end of your dive. The most important rule here is that you never go faster than 18 meters per minute. A rule of thumb is: never faster than the smallest bubbles of your exhalation. That way you do not get decompression sickness, and you can keep everything under control. Your wetsuit will be expending so you have to let air out of your BCD always running. It is a good and cautious habit to always make a safety stop: you do not go straight to the surface, but you stop at five meters deep, and wait there for three minutes. In this way, even more nitrogen can escape from your body, and you have even less chance of decompression sickness.

You obviously do not just go up like thar, we also have a mnemonic for that,

STARS: Signal, Time, Air (BCD and look up), Reach, Swim

If you then come to the surface, you immediately ensure that you have positive buoyancy before you do anything else. So you always inflate your BCD first! Then you can switch to your snorkel (or just keep your regulator if you want), and finally you give a sign that everything is ok to your buddy and if you dive from a boat, you give a sign to the divemaster of the boat. You can then swim towards it, or the boat will pick you up.

As you know, a wetsuit works by holding a layer of water between your skin and the suit. A drysuit insulates even better, because here a layer of air instead of water is between your skin and your suit. And then you also have snorkel suits, ordinary thin suits that do not insulate at all.

If you dive in the tropics and you wear a wetsuit or a dry suit, you can get pretty hot outside of the water. So you always have to watch out for overheating.

Your dive knife is intended as an instrument to point out things, or in case you are stuck, to cut yourself loose. That is why you should always be able to reach your knife with both hands.

When the visibility is very good, and you go down without a rope it can happen that you are completely in blue, above the bottom left, everything is blue. You can get dizzy. In order to prevent this, it is best to use a line so that you have an orientation point, and look at your depth gauge so that you see how deep you are and how fast you go down. This also applies when you go diving at night, which you can do during your advanced open water.

If you start a dive, and there is current, you start against the current. This way you know for sure that if you turn around halfway to go back, the current will help you to return to your starting point!

If you dive from a boat, and you come up a little from the boat after your dive, you do not have to fight the current. You make sure you float, and then you swim perpendicular to the current to the line that hangs behind the boat (if there is one). You can also signal to the boat so that they can pick you up if necessary

As you now know, you always maintain underwater perfect neutral buoyancy. Not only for yourself, but also because you will not crash into the ground and destroy everything (including yourself), and do not make sand or mud to spoil the visibility.

If the conditions are such that you do not feel confident enough to go diving, do not go diving. It's that simple. You are responsible for your own safety, and you will make that decision, nobody else!

If you go diving in a place you are not familiar with, you need to get all the information you need to dive safely and enjoyable. So you have to talk to people who work there or who often dive there.

You must always stay within your own limits and the limits of your education. If you do not take this into account, you can underestimate the dangers and have a false sense of security. You might get very stressed during your dive if things happen you are not prepared for, and you may panic quicker.

Let's talk about plants and animals under water. They do not interact with us very much. We are not food and no competitors for them, so they prefer to leave us alone. This also applies to sharks, there is nothing to be afraid of. Fish are very predictable in their behaviour, so you rarely come across surprises. If animals underwater interact with you it is because they feel attacked, usually because you swim into their territory. You swim quietly away on your back, your fins towards them, out of their territory and everyone is happy again.

You never touch anything under water. It is best to always wear a suit so that it can protect you. During your orientation you get information about potential dangers, so you are aware of everything. You look carefully where your hands, knees and feet are, and you following these rules to help people with injuries caused by plants or animals:

- Check breathing and heart rate
- Rinse punctures with salt water, and do not rub
- Stings by jellyfish and fire coral: treat with vinegar
- Stings by fish such as scorpion fish, rays: hot water for as long as possible
- Carefully remove sea urchin spikes so that they do not break, otherwise leave this to medical staff
- Clean and dress bleeding wounds
- Monitor for allergic reactions, and in case of large wounds go to medics

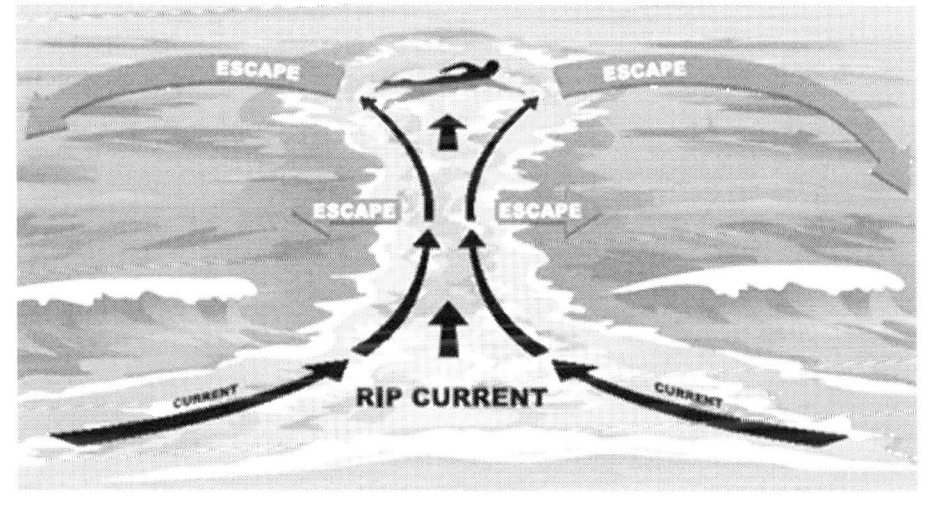

Back to currents. When people drown at the coast, it is usually because they end up in a rip current. A rip current occurs between two sandbanks. When it is high tide, the sandbanks are flooded, and there is no current. When it becomes low tide, the sandbanks obstruct the water that is flowing back to the sea. All the water going towards the sea is squeezed through the narrow passage between the sandbanks, and so there is a strong current with foam away from the coast. The worst thing you can do is trying to swim against that current. Swim at a right angle to the current, parallel to the coast, and this way you swim out of it, away from the hole, and you can go back to the beach. Of course you will have any troubles like when you are diving from a boat!

The influence of the tides can vary greatly between different places. In some places you have twice high and low tide, some places this happens only once, and also the height of high and low tide can be very different in different places. The greater the tides, the more they influence the depths, the strength of the currents, and consequently the visibility.

When you dive from a boat, you will see that there is a roster where a divemaster keeps track of the names of all divers, or at least the number of divers or buddy teams. The boat roster ensures that the divemaster knows where divers are, and no one can be left behind when the boat goes away.

There are different ways to enter the water in your gear. Which one you use depends on the situation. You can usually walk from the coast, you can roll backwards from a dingy, you can step off a larger boat. You always choose the easiest way.

The propeller of a boat is life-threatening for divers. You always stay away as far as possible. Just as you always assume with a pistol that it is loaded, you assume with propeller that it can start moving any moment.

A dive boat that is not moving usually has three lines. The first is the buoy line (anchor line), to which the boat is attached to, and that you can use to go down. The second is the trail line behind the boat, with the current, and that you can use to drag yourself towards the boat at the end of the dive. The third is the swim line that runs from the back to the front of the boat, and that can use you to pull yourself from the back to the anchor line at the front at the beginning of your dive, to go down there on the buoy line.

The first thing you have to do when you come up from a dive, every dive, is to make sure you are floating: inflate your BCD, and if there is a problem, drop your weight belt. Then you can switch to your snorkel if you want, and check with your buddy. You must both be carrying something to signal with if you are lost and cannot see the boat for example. A whistle and a mirror are fine.

And you always stay together, never split up to go searching!

Let's take a look at some emergency situations where you can offer help. The first rule in offering help is always: your own safety first! If you put yourself at risk in helping, you have only made the problem twice as big. Always look first: am I safe, and how do I keep myself safe? Let's look at a diver with a problem on the surface. They are either in responsive or not. Responsive divers you can help by talking and you can approach them immediately. Divers who are not responding are panicking. They have not inflated their BCD, have big round eyes, their masks are gone or on their foreheads, and they beat around their arms. What you have to do first is to provide positive buoyancy for yourself AND the diver, and doing so without endangering yourself. You inflate your own BCD, and do not hesitate to throw away your own weight belt if necessary. The best way to help the diver is to throw a float at them, so that they can cling on to that (and not to you!) If that is not possible, approach the diver very carefully, with you regulator in and your mask on, and help them by inflating their BCD and dropping their weight belts. But stay out of reach, and try to approach from behind or from underwater.

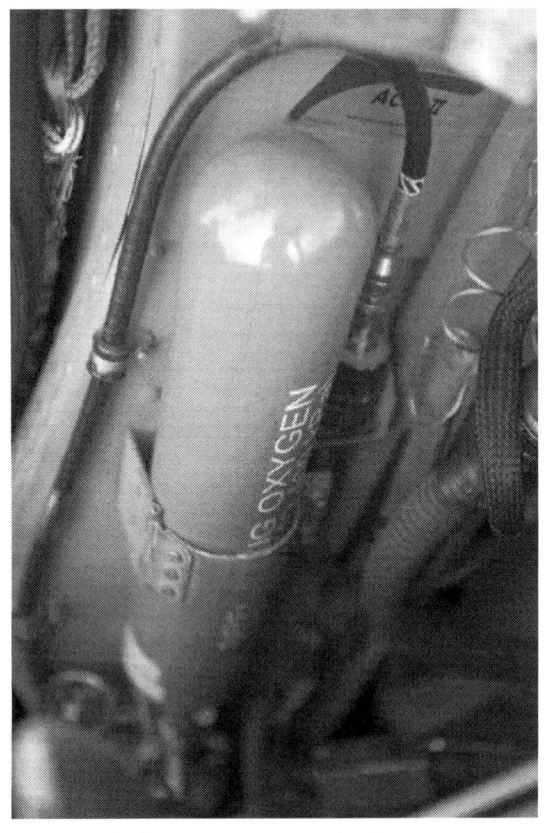

If divers do not move and do not respond, they are unconscious. The very first thing you have to do immediately is to bring that diver to the surface, of course, if you are underwater. If they have their regulator in their mouth, fine, if they do not, it does not matter: bring them straight away to the surface! Inflate the diver's BCD with small amounts during the ascent if necessary, on the surface drop the weight belt during the ascent, but you certainly do that when you're on the surface. When you are up, you have to call for help, check breathing and heartbeat, and if necessary start with mouth-to-mouth resuscitation (keep the victim's nose closed!). And while you do this pull the diver goes towards the shore or towards the boat. Do not worry about doing everything just right, but do something. Everything you do is better than doing nothing!

What should you do if you become tired under water yourself, and get out of breath? Then you do not have to go up, but you have to give your buddy a sign, and rest until you catch your breath.

The first thing you do in any diving accident with a physical problem, such as near-drowning, being unconscious, after you have ensured that the diver is breathing give them pure oxygen. Straight away. Always.

Let's talk about what to do if you have almost no or even no more air under water. You have a few options. If you still have enough to reach the surface, you can of course just go up. If you do not have enough, and your buddy is near you, you will use the alternative air source of your buddy, and you go up together. But suppose that for some reason your buddy is too far away the surface is closer than your buddy, and you're not deeper than 9/10 meters? Then you will do a Controlled Swimming Emergency Ascent (CESA). This is just swimming up as you slowly exhale by saying aaaaaaah in your regulator. If you think you will not make it to the surface, or you are deeper than 9/10 meters, you can also drop your weight belt. In this case, your ascent is no longer controlled, and you do an ascent with positive buoyancy, so that you are sure that you are getting the surface.

When a diver who has had an accident, such as near drowning, being unconscious or being suspected of decompression sickness has been given oxygen they should always be brought to medical help, even if they seem to have been completely recovered. Giving oxygen = bringing to doctor.

Boats are dangerous for divers. Even if you have a buoy, a dive flag or whatever on the surface, always stay deep enough when you can hear a boat so that you can never get hit.

If you clean up things under water and put them in a net, you have to make sure you can just throw that net away if there is a problem. That's why you should not tie it to your equipment

You should not go diving if you have a cold, even if it is only a little bit, because it can cause problems with equalising.

Take care that you are in reasonable condition and be careful if you have heart disease. Exercise, overheating, climbing a ladder and walking with your equipment can cause a heart attack and other cardiovascular problems

Of course it makes sense that you do not drink alcohol before diving. The same is true for taking medicines that impair your judgment and make you drowsy. You should not smoke either, especially a few hours before and after a dive, because your lungs are extra vulnerable at this time. Because there is not enough research on pregnancy and diving, you should not go diving if you are pregnant. And finally: you have to keep up your skills: if you have not been diving for six months or more, you need to do a refresher course.

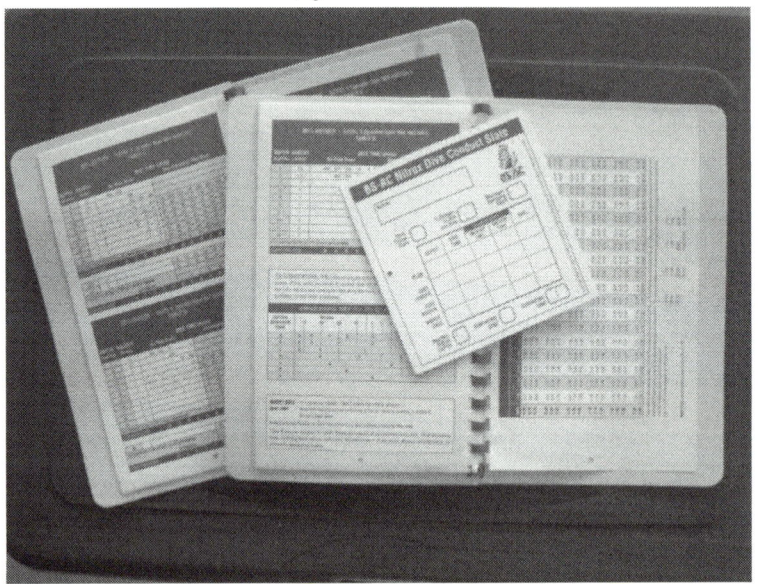

The air you breathe consists of 79% nitrogen and 21% oxygen. If you inhale too much nitrogen under pressure, bubbles may form in your body. These can then cause decompression sickness. This happens when the bubbles block the blood flow, and you experience symptoms such as numbness, weakness and tingling in arms and legs. This is getting slowly worse over the course of hours, so it is not an emergency: you have enough time to seek medical help. If you think someone has decompression sickness, then you give pure oxygen, as always, and go to medical help.

You avoid decompression sickness by not diving too long and not too deep, and we have tables and computers for that. Some secondary physical things increase the chance of decompression sickness. They are quite logical because they all have to do with your circulatory system and condition: fatigue, illness (also colds), older age, alcohol use, heavy physical exertion after and during the dive, dehydration, bad condition, too high weight and injuries.

Sometimes divers use enriched air (nitrox). That's a trick to be able to dive for longer: you take a part of the nitrogen from your tank, and you put oxygen in its place. This way you breath in less nitrogen and you can dive longer.

But too much oxygen is also not good: oxygen becomes poisonous when you get the equivalent of 140 percent (so with 7 bar, around sixty meters deep so when you dive with ordinary air) When you dive with enriched air, say 40 percent oxygen and 60 percent nitrogen, then you already have a problem much shallower. With twice as much oxygen in your tank as normal air contains you can only go up to 30 meters deep! Never go diving with enriched air without training. You can learn to dive with nitrox during your advanced open water. You now also will understand that you should never dive with pure oxygen!

For your third and fourth dive we will go up to 18 meters deep. Do you remember how much the pressure was at 20 meters? Right, 1 bar of the air, and 2 of the water, so a total of 3 bar. That means that every breath you take at that depth counts for three. In other words, you get three times as much air in your lungs (and your tank is empty three times as quickly). The air in your tank is ordinary air, about 80 percent nitrogen and 20 per cent oxygen. That means that when you are diving 20 meters deep (3 bar), it feels to your body as if you get 3 times as much nitrogen (240 percent) and 3 times as much oxygen (60%). And suppose there was 2 per cent carbon monoxide or any other contamination in your tank. Then at 20 meters it feels like 6 per cent, and that's a problem (carbon monoxide poisoning recognizes cherry red lips, headaches, dizziness) So you want to be sure that you have pure air in your tank, and the only way to do that is by filling your tank at a recognized filling station.

Let's take a closer look at how long and how deep you can dive. The time that you can dive to a certain depth at a certain depth without risking decompression sickness is called your no-stop limit (no-decompression limit). If you are going to dive any longer, you should make decompression stops, which is no longer recreational diving. In recreational diving you can always go directly up to the surface, and you never dive longer than your no-stop time.

Your no-stop time is less than when you dive deeper, and your no-stop time of your second or third dive is also shorter than the dive before: you already have some nitrogen in your body when you start with a second or third dive. The recommendation is that if you make multiple dives, the first dive is your deepest.

No-stop times for every depth and every repetitive dive can be found in tables, but we often use a dive computer. It keeps track of how long you are at which depth and how long you were on the surface between dives, and gives exactly the number of minutes you can stay at the depth you are diving. A computer therefore indicates your personal dive profile, so you have to use the same one all day, and not share it with a buddy. You have to stay well within the limits, and it is smart to use the most conservative computer if your buddy uses a different computer. If your computer breaks down under water, that of course means the end of your dive.

But a computer does even more. To prevent decompression sickness you also have to go up slowly after a dive, so that the pressure does not change too quickly, and no bubbles can occur (you already knew that). A dive computer will beep if you go too fast. A dive computer also monitors your safety stop: that is a stop when you are going up of three minutes at five meters to reduce the risk of decompression sickness. It is advisable to always make one if you can.

If you want to make several dives a row, you need to know how long you need to stay on the surface to make your second dive to the depth and the dive time you want. This is the calculation of a surface interval. You can do that in four ways. You can of course just wait and keep looking at your computer until the no-stop time is what you want. There is also a special planning mode on your computer, so you can immediately see how long you have to wait. There are also special diving apps that you can use, and you can also use the old-fashioned table or an electronic version.

This is also concern with flying after diving. We use the following rules for flying after diving: after one dive you have to wait at least 12 hours, after 2 dives or more you wait 18 hours

As mentioned above, diving at altitude, in lower air pressure, requires special procedures (because the pressure differences are greater if you start with less pressure). We keep a height of 300 meters for normal diving, higher than that you need special procedures

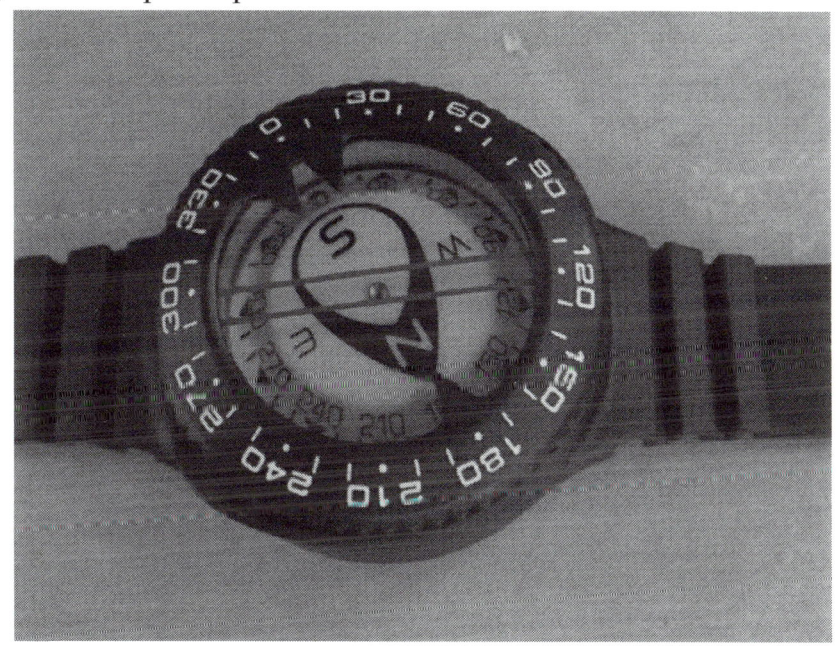

If you dive in the cold or exercise a lot during a dive, you breathe more, and you also get more nitrogen in your body. You can take that into account by setting your computer to a safer position or staying well within your no-stop times.

If you go beyond your no-stop time by accident, you must do an emergency stop. That is just like a regular safety stop on five meters deep, but now you stay there instead of three minutes as long as your computer indicates.

If you had to do emergency decompression stop, but you did not, and you are already on the boat you NEVER go back into the water. You stay on the surface, breathing pure oxygen and you check for symptoms of decompression sickness.

If you do not have enough air to make the whole emergency decompression stop as your computer indicates, you stay for as long as you can, but you keep enough air to make a normal, safe ascent to the surface.

If someone has decompression sickness you: monitor breathing, warn medical service, keep them lying down, and give oxygen until medical assistance is available.

The treatment of almost every case of decompression sickness is a stay in a recompression chamber.

**When you dive around thirty meters or deeper you can get gas narcosis.** It feels like drunkenness, light in your head, and you have problems with concentration and thinking. It is not dangerous in itself, and if you go up a bit it immediately disappears.

A compass has a floating needle that points to the north: the magnetic north needle. There is line right through the middle that represents the direction in which you are swimming: the lubber line. All around are heading references (10, 20, 30 ... 350). You can turn it and there is an index mark on it: the bezel: the index mark. If you want to swim a straight course, keep your compass perfectly horizontal, and point the lubber line (and yourself with it) in the direction you want to swim. You let the magnetic north needle stabilize. Then you turn the adjusting ring so that the bezel is exactly over the north needle, and you hold the needle on the bezel while you swim.

Printed in Great Britain
by Amazon